The
Perfect
Dismissal

GW00802176

THE PERFECT SERIES

ALL YOU NEED TO GET IT RIGHT FIRST
TIME

OTHER TITLES IN THE SERIES:

The Perfect Dismissal

ALL YOU NEED
TO GET IT RIGHT
FIRST TIME

JOHN McMANUS

ARROW
BUSINESS BOOKS

Published by Arrow Books in 1994

3 5 7 9 10 8 6 4 2

Copyright © John McManus 1993

John McManus has asserted his right under the Copyright, Designs and
Patents Act, 1988 to be identified as the author of this work.

First published in Great Britain by
Century Business
an imprint of Random House UK Limited
20 Vauxhall Bridge Road, London SW1V 2SA

Random House Australia (Pty) Limited
20 Alfred Street, Milsons Point, Sydney,
New South Wales 2061, Australia

Random House New Zealand Limited
18 Poland Road, Glenfield
Auckland 10, New Zealand

Random House South Africa (Pty) Limited
PO Box 337, Bergvlei, South Africa

Set in Bembo by
SX Composing Ltd., Rayleigh, Essex
Printed and bound in Great Britain by
Cox & Wyman Ltd, Reading, Berks

British Library Cataloguing in Publication Data
A catalogue record for this book is available from
the British Library

Random House UK Limited Reg. No. 954009
ISBN 0–7126–5641–3

ABOUT THE AUTHOR

John McManus FCIS FIPM is MD of John Courtis &
Partners, a long established management search and
selection consultancy. His 30 year experience in manu-
facturing and service industries has spanned the development of much of today's employment law. His
background in general management and senior staff
roles, in union and non-union environments, brings an
unusually wide perspective and insight to a complex
area of labour law and human relations.

CONTENTS

FOREWORD

No-one I've ever met, who had been fired, ever used the word perfect to describe what happened to them. So this book will seem to be written for employers. Indeed it is: but if you are likely to be a receiver rather than a giver of bad tidings, read on. If a dismissal is handled badly, it might cost the employer some money – sometimes a lot of money.

Employment law is designed more to protect the employee than the employer. That's right and proper: the employee is reckoned to have a lot less clout. But the employer retains one inarguable right. If he doesn't want someone around the place any more, he can fire him. It might be expensive in the event, but that's his right.

Inevitably much of what follows concerns itself with the avoidance of legal pitfalls and the associated costs. Yet there will be other considerations. They concern good practice, common sense, fairness, humanity and the dignity of the individual. It may not be possible to translate these words into cash equivalents, but they are nonetheless important. How much is your corporate reputation worth?

John McManus

INTRODUCTION

It's very tiresome being told that prevention is better than cure: especially when things have gone wrong already and we are looking for some way to retrieve the situation. We all know that we are supposed to act calmly, dispassionately, fairly, even-handedly and all the rest of it. But, when the blood is up, or when we have forgotten to engage brain, sometimes we don't.

Herein you will discover – if you haven't found out already – that, if you have acted carelessly or in anger, there may be a price to pay which, with hindsight, you would rather have avoided. Let's say it now, maybe the best you can hope for is damage limitation.

Wrestling with any problem in this area will be a little easier if you understand something of the background to Employment Law. Unlike those countries with a codified legal system, we have depended until recently on our Common Law – in effect on judges' decisions in specific cases which established precedents which bound inferior courts. Not surprisingly perhaps, these decisions tended to favour the employer. One judge, remarking on the master and servant relationship which seemed to be implied, likened it to a Tsar's attitude to his serfs.

The concept of unfair dismissal was established originally by the now superseded Industrial Relations Act 1971. Until then an employer could dismiss any employee, subject only to a period of notice which had been agreed earlier, or what was seen to be reasonable notice in the event. The employer could escape even this liability if the employee had acted in some way which struck at the heart of the employment contract.

The word reasonable, by the way, is going to appear in

these notes more often than one might like. And the only way either party in a dispute will be able to find out what it means is to ask a judge or an employment tribunal. Elsewhere you'll get what amounts to mere opinion.

It is important to distinguish between **wrongful dismissal** and **unfair dismissal**.

Wrongful dismissal

This is the label applied under common law. From the employee's point of view, the remedies supplied by the courts have not been traditionally attractive. They have been more or less limited to an award of a payment in respect of notice. The courts do not generally set out to establish the fairness or lack thereof of the employer's actions. Neither will they order him to give an ex-employee his or her job back.

Having said this, the common law route may still be attractive for higher paid employees. Current statutes tend to establish relatively low limits for compensation. A court, as opposed to a tribunal, may take a more realistic view of potential loss of earnings for example. It may be possible too, via the courts, to obtain an injunction preventing dismissal in certain circumstances.

Unfair dismissal

The statutory definition this time: with the spectre of Industrial Tribunals looming in the background as the words are uttered. Yet employees have not fared well in this arena in recent years, with a success rate below 40 per cent.

These Tribunals and the superior Employment Appeal Tribunal were supposed to represent an informal, cheap but rarely cheerful way of settling disputes. Over the last 16 years or so they have built up a body of case law of their own. Employers and employees alike have found it necessary to be legally represented at hearings in many instances. It probably wasn't a cheap way to settle things for them.

Some experts in this area might argue that tribunals have lost their way. They are supposed to concern themselves with facts and to settle claims. Instead they have become legalistic, spending much of their time in settling fine legal points and niceties. The Court of Appeal, in some dismay, has set about remedying this. It is a complex area however; even the Court of Appeal's new guidelines raise question marks.

WHEN IS A DISMISSAL A DISMISSAL?

An employee's claim of unfair dismissal or for redundancy payment depends upon one thing above all else. He or she must have been dismissed. This sounds obvious, but it is possible, in certain circumstances, for the employer to argue that dismissal has not taken place: that, however the job ended, it did not amount to dismissal. If the employer can show that this is the case, the employee's cause fails then and there.

Before moving to the exceptions, let's look at what *does* constitute dismissal beyond any doubt:

TERMINATION DEEMED TO BE DISMISSAL

- conventional dismissal by notice
- dismissal for serious breach of contract
- wrongful dismissal
- an act by the employer or any event affecting the employer (including death, partnership dissolution or winding up of a company) which has the effect of terminating the contract will be deemed a dismissal for redundancy purposes.
  (note that this definition concerns the employee's

protection under employment statute rather than common law).
- termination of the contract by the employer with or without notice
- failure to renew a fixed term contract
- when constructive dismissal has occurred, i.e. when the employee is entitled to terminate it by reason of the employer's conduct

and now, the other side of the coin.

TERMINATION *NOT* INVOLVING DISMISSAL

- death or dissolution of the employer. (No, this is not a contradiction. This time the definition concerns the difference between unfair dismissal and redundancy.)
- expiry of fixed term contracts
- frustration – which will be defined at a later stage
- mutual agreement

WRITTEN REASONS FOR DISMISSAL

Any employee who has been dismissed or is under notice of dismissal has the statutory right to be provided with a written statement of reasons for the dismissal. The employer has 14 days in which to produce it. This statement is admissable within tribunal proceedings. It is very important that the reasons given to the employee and the tribunal should be the same.

If the employer fails to provide a statement on request, the employee can complain to a tribunal. The tribunal will then decide what the reasons were – and award two weeks' wages to the employee. This routine need not be necessarily connected with any claim of unfair dismissal: it merely reflects the employee's right to know why he or she has been fired.

The employer's statement does not need to follow any

specified format. Quoting earlier correspondence is adequate – provided copies are attached. Curiously, at first sight anyway, the employer's reasons do not have to be factually correct. It is sufficient that he believed when he wrote it that what he said was correct.

We don't need any more definitions at this stage. The next chapter describes the means by which the employer ought to build his defences. Be warned: the process begins before the employee sets his first paid footstep over the employer's threshold.

BUILDING THE EARTHWORKS

CONDITIONS OF SERVICE

Any lawyer will tell you that a formal, written contract, whatever it concerns, only really comes into its own when things go wrong. He'll tell you too that contracts do not have to be in writing: oral contracts bind just as much. There's an old saying which runs, Put your trust in God: but get it in writing.

The employer's job offer letter forms part of the employee's contract of service. So does what the employer said during the courtship dance we call recruitment. If the employee was misled by what was said at interview or by the terms of the offer letter, he has a legitimate grievance, which he may be able, later, to turn to his advantage.

THE FORMAL EMPLOYMENT CONTRACT

Parliament has established by statute that an employee is entitled to receive minimum written particulars of his contract of employment within 13 weeks of his or her start date. The minimum required is:

1. **Name of employer.** Be careful: in a group it's easy to forget which company is the employer.
2. **Employee's job title.** Some jobs carry titles which are not self-explanatory. If necessary, explain it; and mention major tasks if, once again, they may not be readily inferred.
3. **Date of start of employment.** Don't be vague. Precision may matter later on.
4. **Whether or not employment is continuous.** In the event of a takeover or, say, the transfer of an employee to an associated company, continuity,

or lack of it, is important in relation to pension rights, redundancy and period of notice required.

5. **Remuneration.** Salary/wage, commission or bonus. It is important to state the method of calculation, what is basic pay, how much is cost of living allowance, whether or not there is compulsory overtime, the fact that travel allowances do not form part of pay and any other element which may exist. Remember that there will be a need for clarity when dismissal is involved. The final pay packet comes under intense scrutiny.

6. **Fringe benefits.** For example, car, share options, season ticket loans, subsidised canteen, private medical cover, subsidised mortgage.

7. **Hours of work.** Allow maximum flexibility. Because a worker starts on night shift, don't presume you'll want him there forever. If overtime is compulsory, or guaranteed, say so. Lateness may be difficult to prove if the contract does not specify hours of work. Compulsory overtime deserves mention here too.

8. **Holidays and holiday pay.** When does the leave year start? At what rate do holidays accrue? When must they be taken and in what maximum lumps? May holidays be carried over from one leave year to the next if untaken? Is there a booking mechanism: who may approve/disapprove?

It's worth noting that there is no automatic right to holidays. Beyond Bank Holidays the law does not require employers to provide paid or unpaid holidays. If the employer is silent on the subject however, tribunals and courts would take the company's custom and practice as the rule.

(Many employers choose to issue a separate document dealing with this subject. Do so by all means; but don't forget to give it to the employee.)

9. **Place of work.** If the employer anticipates that he may need to move the employee to another location at a later date, he should say so at the outset. If

he does not and the move is more than just local, he might be judged to have dismissed the employee in effect. His action might amount to constructive dismissal or redundancy, both of which are dealt with in more detail later.

10. **Sick pay.** As with holidays, there's no automatic right, other than to Statutory Sick Pay. Here is the opportunity to say, for example, that there is no entitlement in the first six months, that payment is discretionary for the next 18 months and is limited to six weeks in any 12 months thereafter, or whatever else the employer has established as his policy. It's important to set out the method of calculation too, e.g. the employer offers to make up the difference between actual or deemed SSP and the employee's basic wage – or, say, average earnings over the last 12 weeks – or whatever the formula. *Above all, if there is no sick pay scheme, say so. Silence may be very expensive.*

11. **Pension rights.** All that needs to be set out at this point is that the employer's scheme is contracted in or out of the scheme. There's more to be said on the subject of pensions later though. *As in the case of sick pay, if there are no pension arrangements, the employer must say so. If he does not, he might find himself involved in considerable expense.*

12. **Grievance procedure.** An employee needs to know to whom he should go if he believes he has been unfairly treated.

13. **Disciplinary rules.** The best contracts refer to *an easily accessible document* which sets out not only the grievance procedure but the employer's detailed policy in this area.

14. **Notice.** How much is the employee entitled to – and what must he or she give? And the employer might as well be realistic here. He might like the employee to give him six months, but would he

really want him or her hanging around that long if they've already got another job to go to?

(Employers should note at this point that there is a substantive difference between contractual periods of notice and those which may be required in cases of dismissal, including redundancy.) The statutory minima are:

Period of continuous service	Required minimum notice
One month or more but under two years.	One week
Two years or more but under twelve years.	One week for each year of continuous service.
Twelve years or more.	Twelve weeks.

So much for the legal requirements. In looking at the list you will have gathered that it represents our lawmakers' assessment of the basic information an employee needs for his or her protection. That's probably a fair view. The careful employer will feel that he needs additional protection for himself. Here are a few additional items that he ought to consider:

15. **Dedication.** The employee must devote himself full time to the employer's business and not engage in any other business or employment without the employer's prior *express* consent, i.e. consent in writing. You'll need to distinguish between the representative who might be selling other people's goods on your time and the part-timer who needs additional income to survive.

16. **Restraint.** More properly restraint of trade and a restriction on an ex-employee's right to compete after leaving the employer's service; and something of a minefield. The employer may well need

legal help if he is to draft something which will stick. Restraint depends on time and distance: too long or too far and a tribunal or a court would find the attempted restraint unreasonable.

Ultimately it's difficult if not impossible to prevent someone from earning a living by plying their craft. Many employers produce very widely drawn clauses in the hope that their ex-employees will be frightened into compliance. It's largely a waste of time. In these circumstances the former employee can often get quick, relatively cheap advice from a competent lawyer.

17. **Accommodation.** If a house or flat goes with the job, be very careful. It's all too easy to acquire a tenant as distinct from an employee. The occupier must be living there because he or she can do his job better from there; and the contract must say so. Don't try to save money: you need a lawyer to draft this clause.

18. **Secrecy.** Some companies have separate, quite lengthy agreements in this area: it depends on the nature of the business. Whichever route, it needs to be covered from the day the individual starts.

19. **Health and safety.** When an employer uses a particularly hazardous system, process or materials, it will be prudent to require the employee to conform to the company's safety procedures – and to tell him that, if he does not, he may be dismissed. This will not excuse the employer from making sure that the employee gets the full version of the company's rules in this context: it serves to underline the importance the employer attaches to the requirement.

20. **Search.** If it is the company's practice to search the person and property of employees periodically, say so in the contract. It will not remove the need to obtain the individual's consent at the time, but it has the merit of making the principle clear from the start.

21. **Special terms.** Any other special rules which relate to particular jobs or individuals.

As a matter of interest, an employer cannot make a binding agreement with a *new* employee to the effect that the employee will not claim against him for unfair dismissal or redundancy rights. The newcomer might sign it, but it would be useless in law – unless there is a fixed-term contract for one year or more.

THE LESS OBVIOUS PARTS OF THE CONTRACT OF EMPLOYMENT

The employer/employee contract consists of a lot more than the minimal document which is required to be produced within 13 weeks of the new employee's arrival. It's pointless to delay its issue too, by the way. Employers ought to aim at producing it within days rather than weeks.

The promises made, the indications given by the employer during the recruitment and selection process form part of the contract. Remember that oral contracts are binding too. Conversely the employer cannot slip into the formal document little nasties that he claims to have forgotten to mention in the early stages, like membership of the executive share option scheme is available to the job holder – but there's a five year qualifying period he neglected to mention at the time.

Of course there's a lot more to the bargain which has been struck between the two parties than is immediately obvious. Like an iceberg, four-fifths, or whatever the fraction is, lurks beneath the surface. Let's look at the titles of some of the documents which ought to and probably do exist in most cases, which bear on the whole employment contract:

Disciplinary code
Grievance procedure
Company rules, general and local
Pension Fund rules
Health and safety policy
Redundancy policy
Profit sharing/bonus scheme rules
Share option scheme rules
Private medical cover policy
Holidays/sickpay re long service
Staff loans

A number of these headings will be dealt with in more detail at a later stage. For the moment let's concentrate on the simple issue of getting the information to the employee – not for fun, not because the employer is merely pedantic – but because, when dismissal is involved, the employer will be at a significant disadvantage if he cannot demonstrate that he has given the fullest information to the employee or at least made it very easily available.

There's a simple way to do this. Establish a formal *Induction Process* and make it the direct responsibility of one person in the organization. The Personnel Manager or Company Secretary will be obvious choices. And then make sure that someone audits them to make sure it is done. The system must not be allowed to slip into disuse.

The process centres on a check list. It is possible to buy commercially prepared forms on NCR paper but it is not too difficult to construct one's own version. At the end of, say, the employee's first week the appointed person sits down with the newcomer and they run through the list together. If he or she has not got copies of the documents mentioned, they will be given to him then and there. If this is not practicable, as in the case of the pension fund trust deed and rules, he or she will be told when, where and how they can gain access.

The various items are checked off with a series of ticks and the employee, finally, signs the list acknowledging the completion of the process – which might take up no more than five or ten minutes or a little longer if explanations are needed. Thereafter the employee gets the bottom copy: the top one goes into his or her personnel file. Easy; and worth a little bit of trouble. It's cheap insurance.

2

REDUNDANCY

Chapter 1 dealt with the construction of the employer's basic defences against accusations of wrongful or unfair dismissal. Dismissal by reason of redundancy is by far the most common category he will encounter. The employer will need a thorough grasp of the principles involved. As this review unfolds it is hoped that the preparatory work suggested earlier will seem less like the counsel of perfection and more like just good sense. The store of background knowledge will be added to later but, for the moment, let's take a look at the practical issues of redundancy.

WHEN HAS IT TAKEN PLACE?

The Employment Protection (Consolidation) Act 1978 says that an employee is dismissed by reason of redundancy if the dismissal is wholly or principally because:

- the employer has ceased, or intends to cease, to carry on the business for the purposes of which the employee was employed
- the employer has ceased, or intends to cease, to carry on that business in the place where the employee was so employed
- the requirements of that business for employees to carry out work of a particular kind have ceased or diminished or are expected to cease or diminish
- the requirements of that business for employees to carry out work of a particular kind in the place where he or she was so employed have ceased or diminished or are expected to cease or diminish

There's a shorthand version. An employee is redundant, if the whole or part of a business is closed – or if it needs fewer people to do the available work.

WHO HAS TO DO THE PROVING?

Invariably, the employer. Sometimes an employer will want to prove that a dismissal was *not* due to redundancy: that, for example, the employee shot himself in the foot and had resigned in the event. To paraphrase the Act, *the employer* must show that a dismissal is not due to redundancy. If he cannot, it will be presumed that it is. It's worth knowing that the employer does not have to prove his case beyond reasonable doubt, merely that the balance of probability is in his favour. But, as is the general rule in employment law, if it looks like being a draw, statute requires a decision in favour of the employee.

SELECTION FOR REDUNDANCY

We'll come back to the business of making sure that the employer is not mistaken in believing that he can declare redundancies. For the moment, let's look at the selection process.

If trade unions, staff associations or employee representatives are involved, they'll need to be consulted. The employer needs to talk to them about – but not necessarily agree with them – the criteria for selection, before they are put into practice.

THE SELECTION CRITERIA

Consistency is important. The application of one set of rules in one part of the organization and another set elsewhere is asking for trouble. The employer must be seen to be even-handed and objective in this approach. Typically he might begin with a list including:

- length of service
- skills
- experience
- attendance/timekeeping record

He might wish to add to this list. It might occur to him

that this is a golden opportunity to get rid of the people who have fallen foul of the company's disciplinary code in the past. If so, he'd be best advised to be cautious. These individuals' past offences may be spent. If there is anything current in the files and the man or woman involved is serving out a probationary period, there's still no valid justification for inclusion in the list. After all, they are still on the books. If the offence was that serious, why weren't they dismissed when it happened?

Length of service

Trade unions will rarely argue with last in, first out. It's a matter of fact. Some of their members won't like it, but the union will have little trouble in defending its position. If only a part of an organization is affected, however, the long-serving employee who transferred there two weeks earlier will not thank them.

The message is clear. Even the snappy, familiar LIFO formula can be treacherous. Think, define: if only one department is affected, is it fair to restrict redundancies to it alone? Should the net be cast wider? Should there be agreed exclusions – like the man who transferred there only recently?

That's not all. LIFO might have the effect of removing skilled workers the employer cannot afford to lose. The attractions of the easy to agree method may be more apparent than real.

Skills/experience

Marketing men speak lovingly of product mix. Companies need a skills and experience mix too. It is common sense for the employer to define the skills and experience he needs to retain to keep his business alive and flourishing and to derive his selection criteria from this analysis. A word of warning however. He must be seen to be fair. His criteria ought to relate to functions and to skill and experience within these functions rather than to individual personalities. It may be possible for him to defend individual preferences in the event: but he'd better have his case well prepared.

Which bring us to **bumping**, i.e. creating a redundancy further along the chain, say because the employer wants to hang on to skilled individuals. Suppose there's a skilled machinist and the employer turns him into a storekeeper pro tem and proceeds to make the storekeeper redundant instead. If the selection criteria were widely drawn in the first instance, this may be a good move for the employer and the machinist. Both will anticipate his return to his original job when business improves. Only the storekeeper will be unhappy.

Bumping is legitimate: but it must not be used as an obvious means of getting rid of individuals who were not much good at their job. If that was the employer's motive and it can be shown to be such, the plan will misfire. The employer will be found to have unfairly dismissed these people.

Attendance/timekeeping

The problem with using attendance and timekeeping records as a basis for selection for redundancy is that the employer is forcing himself to react to a row of figures without regard to the circumstances which created the figures. If an employee had been late on a number of occasions over a three month period because her mother was seriously ill and she had to wait for the nurse to arrive, are these grounds for dismissal?

Once the criteria have been settled, they must be applied without discrimination. Is there a real difference between her and the girl with the same sort of record who has been suffering from morning sickness? Or the man with a similar pattern of absence who may or may not have been ill?

What, for that matter, is an unacceptable level of absence from work? It's an emotive area. There are too many questions and not enough answers. On balance employers would be well advised to steer away from this criterion. There are other ways of dealing with problems of attendance and timekeeping within a well constructed disciplinary code. Redundancy is not the solution.

Unfair selection

Dismissal via redundancy is going to be found unfair when the method of selection:

(a) cuts across a specific agreement with the union or staff.

(b) is in breach of custom and practice within the organization.

(c) concerns a trade union: because of the employee's:

- proposed or actual membership of a union
- taking part or proposing to take part in the activities of a union
- non-membership, refusing or proposing to refuse to become or remain a member of a union

(d) is discriminatory on grounds of sex or race.

(e) has been incorrectly applied to an individual when other employees with the same profile have been ignored.

(f) is aimed, wholly, or in part, at the dismissal of pregnant women.

There have been instances where lack of consultation with individual employees has provided justification for their selection being labelled unfair. He or she might want to make it known that they have other skills: or that they are prepared to work at another location, for example. The phrase used by tribunals is usually 'lack of procedure'.

CONSULTATION
Employers have a statutory duty to consult (Employment Protection Act 1975) with a trade union, *if it has negotiating rights*. The test is not whether the employer thinks it has these rights, but if he negotiates with it on:

- terms and conditions of employment
- union membership
- disciplinary matters, including termination and suspension
- facilities for union activities
- recruitment

The employer is required to give the union written information: meetings and conversations are not enough. In fact consultation has not begun until written information is handed over. It must not be merely for the sake of form: there has to be real opportunity for the union to influence management's views, even if it fails in the event.
- The union must be given reasonable and adequate time to consider management's proposals. *From the employer's point of view timing is critical*. The Act sets out minimum consultation periods and specifies the information to be given to the union:

Minimum consulting period
- 90 days if 100 or more employees will be made redundant in 90 days or less
- 30 days if 10 or more employees will be made redundant in 30 days or less

Disclosure
- the reasons for what is proposed
- the description and the numbers of employees involved

- the totals of employees within the descriptions at the place involved
- the proposed selection criteria
- the method planned, including the period over which dismissals will take effect

An anticipated drop in morale will not constitute a valid reason for failure to consult: neither will ignorance of the statutory requirement – nor contrary advice, from whatever source, *however official it may seem*.

Representations

The law requires employers to consult and to take due note of the representations made by unions. *It does not require the parties to agree.* Nonetheless employers should be advised to treat union suggestions and recommendations seriously and to respond to them constructively and *in writing*. A written record of the exchange may prove to be most useful after the event.

SUBSTANTIVE REASONS FOR REDUNDANCY

The shorthand version suggested earlier said that an employee is redundant if the whole or part of a business is closed or if fewer people are needed to do the work available. Let's pick this apart and look at the implications.

Closure (purpose)

When an entire business is closed, the employer will rarely be asked to justify himself. The industrial tribunal will accept the inevitable.

A business may close down only to spring forth again, but in a different style, demanding different skills of its workers. If this is the case, the re-birth will not help those made redundant earlier. But if mere reorganization is implied and the business remains substantially the same and operates from the same place, redundancy may well be judged as both contrived and ineffective.

Closure (place)

Closing down an uneconomical unit is obviously reasonable and legitimate. Employers are required to provide alternative employment if they can. If there is another site within a reasonable distance, this may well be feasible. For certain employees, salesmen for example, a move to another part of the country may be appropriate. But what if the employee rejects the offer? Is he still redundant? Is he entitled to redundancy payment?

If it is put to the test an industrial tribunal would ask first what the employment contract said about mobility. If the employee refuses to move within the terms of this agreement, his refusal amounts to misconduct. He is not redundant and may be fairly dismissed. If a house move is required when the employment contract is silent, he remains redundant and entitled to payment.

The tribunal in what might be termed local cases, seeks to establish that the employee is being offered a *reasonable* alternative job. It will take into account economic factors such as travel costs, the rewards available for the new job compared with the old and so on. It will then examine the personal and social issues involved. Can the man do this new job? Will he need training; will the employer provide it? Will his age, health, family circumstances militate against it? And, once again the awful word, is it reasonable?

Work of a particular kind

The introduction of *new technology* may result in a need for fewer people – or the same number but with different skills. Technological redundancy is an established reason for dismissal, even when the employees dismissed are replaced immediately – provided, of course, that the newcomers have the new skills required.

Reorganization can produce redundancies too. An employer may choose to re-allocate duties to make his operation more efficient. If the work to be done by individuals is fundamentally different as a result, the employees concerned are redundant in effect. Equally they may be redundant if reorganization results in a need for fewer people.

Sub-contracting work to an external contractor and creating redundancies as a result is legitimate – even when the contractor engages the former employees to do what amounts to the same work they did when they worked for the original employer.

When the volume of business declines, fewer staff may be needed to carry out *work of a particular kind*. Redundancy is legitimate.

As business falls away an employer may see temporary salvation in cutting out the night shift or in reducing the production week from, say 38 to 25 hours. He may offer the night-shift workers day work. If they refuse his offer they will not automatically be redundant. They'd have to be part of an overall staff reduction to attract this definition. They would be dismissed for some other reason. What did their contract of employment say about transfers to and from night shift?

A substantial reduction in working hours will amount to the creation of redundancy. The staff involved may be re-engaged on the revised basis: but they remain entitled to redundancy payments.

AVOIDING REDUNDANCY, OR MINIMIZING ITS EFFECTS

Industrial tribunals do not seek to measure the employer's efficiency. Despite this, evidence that the employer has been thoughtful, careful, that he has done the best he can to avoid redundancies, will be persuasive, all else being equal. Here's a list of the areas he should have examined before he got to the point of declaring anyone redundant:

- Overtime: is it really necessary?
- Recruitment: should he be taking on new people at this stage?
- Early retirement: maybe some of the people whose 'get up and go' got up and went some time ago would relish it.
- Natural wastage: some people will leave of their own accord, for normal reasons. Don't replace them.
- Temps and casuals: couldn't some of the potentially redundant people do their work?
- Short-time working: unions are used to the idea as a means of averting redundancy. They are likely to go along with it. In a non-union environment the employer needs consent.

TAKEOVERS

One final thought within the area of redundancy. For the vast majority of undertakings it is true that, *when a business is sold, the employees' rights are safeguarded*. The Transfer of Undertakings (Protection of Employment) Regulations 1981 are clear. Employees' contracts transfer automatically to the new owner. If an employee is dismissed by the former or the new owner and the reason for dismissal is the transfer of the business, his or her dismissal is unfair.

3

THE DISCIPLINARY CODE AND COMPANY RULES

The employer who finds himself facing an Employment Tribunal will discover that, in any case involving dismissal, the Tribunal will seek to establish:

- the substantive merits of his action
- its procedural correctness.

Setting aside merit for the moment, it's worth looking at the implications of the phrase 'procedural correctness'. At its heart lies the Disciplinary Code, a formal Code of Practice, first published in 1977. Its declared objectives are to promote order and fairness in the treatment of employees and to help an organization to function effectively. Neither side is likely to argue with these aims. The acute employer however may well see that it is very much in his interests to prepare his in-house disciplinary procedures documentation carefully and to make sure that *all* employees get copies of it. *If his procedures are correctly and fairly drawn, they will represent his first line of defence in many instances.*

There are no prizes for failing to prepare and issue these documents. There is no merit in arguing that the organization is too small to need them. Or in affecting to believe that it does not have disciplinary problems and that the appearance of these papers might persuade employees and managers that they exist. Not issuing them falls under the same heading as refusing to have a will prepared, on the basis that it might tempt providence: or that one is immortal.

Disciplinary procedures are not difficult to prepare. There is available a useful ACAS booklet, *Discipline at*

Work for example, which is intended to complement the Code of Practice itself.

For the moment, let's look at what the Code recommends.

THE OUTLINE CODE OF PRACTICE
Disciplinary procedures should:

(a) be in writing.
(b) specify to whom they apply.
(c) provide for matters to be dealt with quickly.
(d) indicate the disciplinary actions which may be taken.
(e) specify the levels of management which may have the authority to take the various forms of disciplinary action, ensuring that immediate superiors do not have the power to dismiss without reference to senior management.
(f) provide for individuals to be informed of the complaints against them and to be given the opportunity to state their case before decisions are reached.
(g) give individuals the right to be accompanied by a trade union representative or by a fellow employee of their choice.
(h) ensure that, except for gross misconduct, no employees are dismissed for a first breach of discipline.
(i) ensure that disciplinary action is not taken until the case has been carefully investigated.
(j) ensure that individuals are given an explanation for any penalty imposed.
(k) provide a right of appeal and specify the procedure to be followed.

COMPANY RULES
A company's disciplinary code is intended to be a general statement. The corporate policy statement in

relation to Health and Safety at work will be equally general. In a company or group with a number of locations, sometimes carrying on different trades and processes, neither can hope to provide for all the eventualities the employer might foresee. It is legitimate, in these circumstances, to supplement these general documents with sets of local rules. If food processing were involved at a site, a ban on smoking might be imposed, for example: elsewhere there might be, say, a requirement that employees must wear radio-activity detection badges at all times.

Company rules can be applied to particular categories of employees too, and may extend beyond the employee's presence at work. Airline pilots, say, must not consume alcohol for 24 hours preceding a flight. There are examples of rules which might even be labelled idiosyncratic. A company may decree that if any of its managers drinks as little as half a pint of beer at lunchtime, he or she may not come back to work in the afternoon.

When an employee works at a single location it is simple enough to supply him with a copy of the Disciplinary Code and local rules when he joins, as part of the induction programme mentioned earlier. When someone visits many sites or there is a change of location, the employer ought to produce a means of coping with this. The change of location is easier: the new arrival goes through the induction programme as though he or she were a new employee. It may be reasonable to argue that visiting staff and managers are likely to be supervised during their visits.

DISCIPLINARY PROCEDURES IN ACTION

Whenever something happens which bears on the company's procedures in this area, supervisors and managers alike must respond in line with the routines established by the procedures. There's no point in having them otherwise. No excuses: if that is what the Procedure requires, do it – no more and certainly no less. Let's look at a typical set of these routines:

- *Get the facts.* Managers and supervisors must be trained to collect information before the memory dims. Myths can be created overnight. Track down available witnesses – preferably immediately.
- *Suspension.* If the offence *looks* serious, (remembering that nothing is proven yet), a brief period of suspension is possible.

  It will be with pay normally. Disciplinary suspension without pay is normally only possible if written into an employee's service contract. Suspension cannot be used conventionally as a punishment. Its general purpose is to give the employer time to investigate particular circumstances. And his investigation must be completed within a reasonable period. A thoughtful disciplinary procedure will normally specify maximum periods.
- *Interview the alleged offender.* He or she must be given opportunity to state their case, alone or accompanied as they choose – and be told what their rights are within the procedure – before any decision is made or penalty imposed.
- *Oral warnings.* Supervisors, for example, often give verbal warnings for minor infringements. It is important that they should understand the difference between what they regard as an everyday, not particularly serious event and a formal oral warning. If an oral warning is to be an effective part of the disciplinary procedure, the employee must be told that, while it is oral, it is nonetheless formal; and that it is the first stage in the disciplinary procedure. The supervisor's manager must be told because, unless it is recorded at the time or very soon thereafter, it may be difficult to prove that it was ever given: or to recall exactly the form it took.

- *Written warnings.* If the first offence is serious, or there has been a repetition of infringements which resulted in oral warnings, a written warning will be issued. It must:

    (i) State the nature of the offence.
    (ii) Set out the consequences of further offences.
    (iii) Tell the employee what stage in the disciplinary procedure this warning represents.

- *Final warnings.* Invariably written, they will follow the format of any other written warning but it must be made clear to the employee that the consequences of further offence now include dismissal – or whatever else the employer believes to be appropriate, including, for example, a disciplinary transfer.

    The employee will have a right of appeal at all stages of the procedure. He or she must always be given a written statement of any disciplinary action which is proposed.

REASONABLENESS
Whatever sanction the employer may have in mind should always be subjected to a test of reasonableness. A tribunal would certainly ask itself if what was done was reasonable in the circumstances.

VARIATIONS TO DISCIPLINARY PROCEDURES
While there is a very strong argument in favour of applying company procedures in this context without variation, there will be circumstances in which common sense will demand some variation. Obvious examples will include:

- Nightshift workers/employees in remote locations. Because no–one senior enough to approve or disapprove action is present. Or because the employee cannot gain access to his trade union representative.

- Trade union officials. They enjoy special status. Beyond an oral warning it is prudent for the employer to do nothing until he has discussed the matter with a senior trade union representative or a full-time union official.
- Criminal offences. Employees should not be dismissed if they are absent through having been remanded in custody. A conviction might raise considerations, depending on the nature of the offence, as to whether the individual in question is unsuitable for the work in which he or she is engaged. Or it may be that the nature of the offence, for example, has made that person unacceptable to other employees.

APPEALS

The disciplinary procedure will contain rights of appeal. There will exist too a grievance procedure, within the employee's contract of service. Generally speaking, the appeal sequence and timings usually set up within a disciplinary procedure will be faster. It's best to keep them in their separate boxes.

Note. A sample Disciplinary Code is given as Appendix 1.

4

COMMON REASONS FOR DISMISSAL

Redundancy has been examined earlier. This chapter will look at a number of other common reasons for dismissal.

QUALIFICATIONS

Unfortunately it is not uncommon for candidates for a job to hold themselves out as possessing skills or qualifications which they do not have. It may take the employer some time to discover this in some cases. It will not necessarily occur to an employer that he needs to check a qualification said to have been gained 20 years earlier. While membership of recognized professional bodies is easy to establish, the claim of a PhD from an overseas university is likely to go unchallenged. And until the new warehouseman drives the fork-lift truck into a concrete pillar on his second day it may not occur to his boss that perhaps he ought to have asked to see the fork-lift truck driver's certificate of competence the man claimed to have.

If the employer recruited him because he believed the individual to possess qualifications and or competences which that individual claimed to have, but did not, dismissal will be fair – provided that such qualifications and or competences are necessary for the performance of the job.

In the context of newly joined employees who set out to mislead the employer, there's a tip worth remembering. Although middle ranking and senior employees are used to presenting CVs rather than filling in forms, ask them to fill in the employer's standard application form anyway. They can leave the job history section blank except for a note that says 'see CV attached'. The point is that they will have signed the declaration built into the form which certifies that all the information contained in the form – now including the CV – is correct. They will find it impossible to argue at some later date that the CV is not theirs and that somebody has obviously fabricated it.

CAPABILITY

The Employment Protection (Consolidation) Act 1978 defines capability as being assessed by reference to 'skill, aptitude, health or any other physical or mental quality'.

Capability is not a word which trips every day from the tongue of the average employer. He will be more familiar with two phrases which form its major sub-headings:

> Sub-standard work
> Long-term sickness

Both bear examination in some detail:

SUB-STANDARD WORK

The definition of capability may imply that an employee ought to arrive with an inherent capability to do the work for which he or she is employed, with training perhaps but possessed of an underlying inherent aptitude at least. *May* in the preceding sentence looks like a weasel word. So it is. Tribunals and courts spend many unhappy hours interpreting statutes.

If it is assumed that the reason that the employer gives for dismissal is lack of capability, related to an absence of inherent aptitude, tribunals and courts alike will recognize that his assessment is bound to be, in some part anyway, subjective. It may well be impossible for him to be wholly objective. Courts are likely to take the view that it is not necessary for the employer to prove that an employee is *in fact* incapable. It is sufficient that he honestly believes on reasonable grounds that the employee in question is incapable.

In other circumstances an employee may have the capacity to do the work required but is either careless or poorly motivated, or both. A court will tend to react as before. It will want to establish that the employer honestly believes in his allegation of sub-standard work; and that he has reasonable grounds for his belief.

In effect the employer will need to demonstrate that he has carried out a careful investigation. It must go significantly beyond a mere suspicion or gossip to the effect that the individual is incompetent. Employers' views in this area are given considerable weight. Tribunals and courts alike, in the main, have recognized that it is management's job to manage. Businesses cannot afford to employ incompetent staff. While a superficial view of employment law in many areas might seem to suggest that it favours the employee, it is certainly not true here. The view taken is that unfair dismissal law must not be allowed to impede employers unreasonably in the efficient management of their business.

Poor performance
There's a most useful booklet on this topic, available from ACAS. It suggests the following:

- the employee should be asked for an explanation and the explanation checked.
- where the reason is the lack of required skills, the employee should, wherever practicable, be assisted through training and given time to reach the required standard of performance.
- where despite encouragement and assistance the

employee is unable to reach the required standard of performance, consideration should be given to finding alternative work.

- where alternative work is not available, the position should be explained to the employee before dismissal action is taken.
- an employee should not normally be dismissed because of poor performance unless warnings and a chance to improve have been given.
- if the main cause of poor performance is the changing nature of the job, employers should consider whether the situation may properly be treated as redundancy rather than a capability issue.

LONG-TERM SICKNESS

The employee absent through sickness or injury for a considerable length of time presents a problem to the employer which is at once moral and practical. He may well wish to retain him as an employee – to keep him on the books, albeit that entitlement to sick pay has been used up long ago.

Sick pay, by the way, is a financial arrangement. Its existence does not imply that an employee cannot be dismissed before entitlement to sick pay is exhausted. Conversely, the exhaustion of sick pay entitlement does not provide grounds for automatic dismissal.

But, reverting to the example, the employee's work still needs to be done. The employer may have used temporary labour until now, possibly at a premium. A full-time employee would cost a lot less. And keeping the man on the books probably preserves his entitlement to paid holidays. All in all, the employer may reason, the business cannot afford it.

If the absent employee is a member of a trade union the employer knows that the union is bound to try to preserve this individual's job if it can. At least it must do what is possible to help a member who, when he returns to health, may face long-term unemployment. It may be possible to compromise: for dismissal to take place but with the employer's undertaking that the individual will be preferred when he is fit again, if suitable vacancies occur.

Perhaps the employee will never be fit enough to work again. When this is known to be the case it is theoretically and sometimes actually possible for the employer to rely on the *doctrine of frustration* within contract law. A contract is frustrated when one party or the other is unable to fulfil the terms of the contract. Lest that should sound too easy, frustration cannot be applied if it has been self-induced – or has happened as the fault of the party seeking to invoke it.

Sickness – pre-dismissal procedures

Perhaps more so in this delicate area than most, employers are likely to fall foul of tribunals if they have not followed reasonable and adequate procedures. Employers are expected to make an effort to find out what is wrong with the employee. They'll need to talk to him or her first. They may decide that medical opinion represents the best hope they have of getting the information they need. It is not inconceivable that an employee may not know or understand his or her condition.

With the employee's consent, the GP concerned might be approached. Whether or not the doctor will co-operate is a matter for his discretion. A relatively recent statute, The Access to Medical Reports Act 1988, requires an employer to tell an employee that he intends to ask the employee's GP for a report – and to get the employee's consent.

At the same time the Act insists that the employee be informed of the rights listed below:

- the right to refuse consent
- the right of access to the report before and after it is supplied to the employer
- the right to refuse consent to the report being supplied to the employer
- the right to amend the report where it is considered by the employee to be incorrect and misleading.

The last of these rights carries a rider. The doctor concerned can accept or reject the suggested alterations. But, if they are rejected, he is nonetheless bound to include a statement of his patient's views with his report.

Of course an employee may simply deny the employer access. It's more than likely that a tribunal would see his refusal as confirming the employer's beliefs.

COMPANY DOCTORS

A number of companies employ medical practitioners part-time, externally usually, but there may be a fully-fledged industrial health department in some instances. These companies' contracts of employment will commonly include a requirement for the employee to undergo medical examination by the company doctor or another doctor selected by the employer, when he joins. And he must perhaps take part in executive check-up programmes at regular intervals. The contract may go on to say that, in the event of protracted, or maybe even periodic but recurring absence due to sickness, he or she will need to submit to examination by the company's appointed doctor. If this is the case, the provisions of The Access to Medical Reports Act 1988 do not apply.

ALTERNATIVE WORK

It's worth stressing that dismissing a sick employee, if it must be done, should be done with care – and, one hopes, with sympathy for that matter. While tribunals and courts do not set out to deny management's right to manage, as was remarked earlier, they want to be reassured that the employer has behaved properly. Thus far, let's say that he has judged that the company must replace the individual concerned, for sound business reasons. He has established the employee's condition and has the doctor's prognosis. He still has one more hurdle to clear. Is it feasible to provide the employee with alternative work?

He is not required to *create* a new job. But if a job exists which the employee might be able to do and it is not offered to him, a tribunal is likely to take a dim view. The employer will be expected to modify a job too, within reasonable limits, if such modification would make it possible for the individual to do the work. Finally, he is bound to offer an alternative job, even if it carries lower rewards than the employee has received in the past.

ABSENTEEISM

It is extraordinarily difficult to distinguish between genuine absence due to sickness and what amounts to malingering. Self-certification under the Statutory Sick Pay arrangements disposed of a major burden on GPs but had the effect of removing a useful filter so far as the employer is concerned. Having said that, if the complaint was of lower back pain, for instance, the GP was usually unable to confirm or deny its existence.

Meticulously kept absence records are vital in this group. Absenteeism shows up as a pattern, individually and in groups. When it's group absenteeism and it commonly occurs on Mondays or when there's a local football Derby, it's easy enough to detect. In the second instance it isn't too difficult to remedy. Try a local sanction – advance notice that overtime will be withdrawn from everyone absent on the day of the match, for a period of one month, without exception and however good the explanation sounds, for example. Or, if there's no overtime being worked anyway, think of something else – turn the attendance bonus into a reflection of total rather than individual presence, or threaten it.

The Monday morning weariness syndrome, whether concerning groups or individuals, is more of a problem. So too is the employee who has no real interest in his or her work and who takes occasional days off at random because they cannot be bothered to go to work. But, while the employer may be deeply suspicious that this is the case, he is bound to behave constructively. A presumption of guilt and out of hand dismissal will almost certainly misfire.

The routine he ought to adopt follows that mentioned earlier in relation to long-term sickness. The individuals must be interviewed and asked what health problems they have. If self-certificates have been presented, which will be the case almost always, the employer should suggest that he or she should consult their GP for proper investigation of their condition: or that the company will happily pay for the employee to see its doctor. The manager conducting the interview will tell the employee that the company will ask the GP or the company doctor for information, given that the employee, in the case of the GP only, does not object. The interviewer should of course make notes of what was said, for future reference.

The GP, or the company doctor, may find nothing of particular consequence – a minor ailment perhaps and insufficient to keep most people away from work. When the findings are known it will be time to talk to the employee again. It may be appropriate to tell him or her that the job they have exists in a critical area and demands their regular attendance and that, if it cannot be sustained, the employer will have to consider some sort of remedy. The remedies might include a transfer to another, less critical, job, for example, which may or may not pay the same money. This last presumes of course that one is available. The employer's ultimate recourse will be dismissal but he must be sure that:

(a) The level of his response is reasonable *in the circumstances*.
(b) What he has done is *procedurally correct*, i.e. that he has been scrupulously fair in his dealings with the employee and given him or her ample time and opportunity to explain, to seek advice and to improve. And that the proceedings have been faithfully recorded.
(c) He is not picking on one employee in particular when other employees present the same or similar profiles but have been ignored in this context.

ACCUMULATED OFFENCES – OR TOTTING UP

The recommended formal written warning will always include mention of the date on which the offence is considered spent, i.e. the date on which the warning will be removed from the individual's personal file and destroyed. From that date it is as though nothing has ever happened. If an expiry date were not quoted, a tribunal would invent one; so there is no virtue in avoiding the issue.

The point of mentioning this here is that employers, confronted by what they see as the last straw, often imagine that they can dredge up episodes and examples which are too old to be admitted as material by any tribunal. And what if the offences, though recent, are unconnected?

Setting aside time–expired offences, totting up may be practicable. A series of offences, although superficially unconnected, may produce a pattern representing an employee's general carelessness and indifference towards his or her job and the employer. Despite this, the employer must be procedurally correct. The wording of his written warnings must be clear. If he is linking, he must say so and tell the employee why. He must have allowed explanation and given the individual time to improve – all of the things one is used to in company's disciplinary procedures. And he must have told the employee in writing what will happen if he or she does not improve.

Inevitably any decision to dismiss as the result of totting up must concern the seriousness with which the employer regards the accumulation. As ever, his actions must be those of a reasonable employer. A tribunal might be unsympathetic if it felt that he was using a limited series of inconsequential breaches as a means of getting rid of someone he didn't like or whom he regarded as a troublemaker. He might have thought this because the employee had dared to breathe the word union during an overheard tea break conversation in the employer's non-union factory. If the employer had not pursued other employees with similar records with as much zeal, or even at all, his motives might well be questioned.

5

UNCOMMON GROUNDS

This chapter deals with some of the less common grounds for dismissal, including, but not limited to gross misconduct. The latter seems to hold a morbid fascination for students. Managers in industry and elsewhere are less enchanted by it. Nonetheless, let's start at the more dramatic end.

Some examples of gross misconduct appear in the sample Disciplinary Code in Appendix 1 at the back of this book. You will read that employees may be subject to summary dismissal without notice if they are found guilty of any of the offences listed – or any other which might attract the gross misconduct label.

Before proceeding further, there are two points to note:

(i) **Summary dismissal** is always without notice – or payment in lieu of notice. Either is a mistaken kindness and thoroughly undermines the case which justifies the employer's action.
(ii) It is often very difficult to define gross misconduct. The definition which is available is meant to be helpful but sounds merely glib – Any act or behaviour by an employee which fundamentally breaches his or her contract of employment, thereby justifying summary dismissal.

It is possible that the breach may occur away from the employee's place of work: but that it may be nonetheless a breach. But, granted that it is a breach, is it serious enough to warrant summary dismissal? Circumstances alter cases; and, once again, the word reasonable creeps in.

The employer must ask himself whether or not someone else, who was totally impartial and had full knowledge of the background, might not have settled for a formal warning. The issues involved are so easily clouded by personalities, emotions and, because we are human, sometimes downright prejudice. The second and final do-it-yourself test is *to ask oneself whether, after the offence in question, this person's continuing presence at work would be wholly intolerable.*

FIGHTING

When Disciplinary Codes give examples of gross misconduct, fighting is almost always near the top of the list. The threat of automatic or summary dismissal tends to go with its mention. At one level it may be argued that not fighting becomes a condition within an individual's contract of service: that, if he or she does so, they will be sacked. At another, underlining the fact that behaviour of this sort is unacceptable, is fair and reasonable, albeit that the threat may be more apparent than real. When confronted by an actual episode, the employer might be well advised, in practice, to ensure that his response is not reflexive, regardless of what he believes the contractual implications to be. In other words, the action he takes might be contractually sound but be judged to be inequitable at a later date.

It would be more prudent for him to investigate the circumstances, as he would if the alleged offence fell into any other category of misconduct. Was there provocation? Was the employee taking reasonable action to defend himself against unprovoked assault? Summary dismissal without regard for equity may well amount to unfair dismissal.

As an afterthought, fighting elsewhere than on the employer's premises may also count as misconduct, if it can be shown to be work connected.

DRINKING, DRUNKENNESS AND DRUGS

As with fighting, the mere existence of a company rule, whether or not it seems to be a condition of employment, ought not to precipitate automatic dismissal. Most employers will have read published accounts of cases in which the police had great difficulty in proving that a man or woman was drunk or under the influence of drugs, or both. The burden of proof placed on an employer is of course not as heavy. Nonetheless he is required to have reasonable grounds for his beliefs. There's a world of difference between *knowing* that an individual consumed eight to ten pints of beer in two hours and not knowing that the effect was caused in fact by two hay fever tablets and a couple of ill-advised but seemingly innocuous rum and cokes.

The employer's investigation might well follow these lines:

- The employee should *always* be suspended, with pay, until he or she is well enough or sober enough to attend a disciplinary hearing.
- An attempt must be made to obtain specific evidence of the individual's drinking or drug taking and his or her condition thereafter.
- When the employee returns to work, his or her account of the circumstances and background will be called for – and recorded in writing.

An employee's status and position matter in this context. What would be the effects of impairment of judgments he or she is required to make? The nature of the job counts too. Would his or her condition imply risk, to themselves or others?

THEFT AND CRIMINAL OFFENCES

Whenever criminal charges are involved – and presuming the alleged offence to be work-related – an employer is faced with an immediate dilemma. The diligent investigation he might wish to pursue may cut across and even prejudice police procedures and any subsequent case brought against the individual concerned. What must he do? Suspension looks as though it provides one answer. But the case may take months to come to court and, meanwhile, the employer is aware that his custom has never been to suspend without pay.

Fortunately, although this is a notoriously grey area, he is allowed some latitude. If the evidence of his preliminary findings is strong enough to enable him to form a reasonable belief in the guilt of the person concerned, he may dismiss that man or woman. *He is not required to await the outcome of legal proceedings in these circumstances.*

If the accused person were, subsequently, to be found innocent by the court, the employer would not be automatically guilty of unfair dismissal as a result. The function of a tribunal is not to determine the guilt or innocence of an employee. Its task is to assess the fairness or otherwise of an employer's actions.

A determined employer can of course ignore police requests that he should not carry out his own investigations. If he wishes to do so, it's worth a call to the company's lawyers before he launches forth, just in case.

Offences which are not related to work present another problem area. Take two examples. First the case of a man who has not paid alimony in accordance with a court order and who is given a short custodial sentence as a result. And the second, another employee charged in connection with an offence which results in remand which extends for many weeks.

If the first instance a period of suspension, matching

what is a sentence usually measured in weeks, would be appropriate. But if this is the third or fourth time this has happened, the employer might reasonably argue that the accumulated effect renders this man unreliable in terms of his availability for work and that he must be dismissed.

The second case is a matter requiring the employer's judgment. If he knows that remand is likely to be protracted, he might opt for dismissal on grounds of the non-availability of the employee, i.e. frustration. Interestingly, although frustration requires that the event which brought it about was not self-induced, it can be argued legally that it was not the commission or alleged commission of an offence which brought about frustration. Rather it was the judge's decision to remand or convict which did it. On the other hand the employer may take the view that the evidence against his employee is not convincing or simply that he wishes to support the individual involved. Suspension, with or without pay may be the solution. There are no ready answers here. The employer must make his own mind up.

DISHONESTY

The preceding section dealt with matters concerning criminal law. An employer may feel disinclined to involve the police on occasion however. An employee who steals from the petty cash box or the till may be merely summarily dismissed. If so the tests a tribunal would apply would be those which, by now, will be familiar. Did the employer genuinely believe in the guilt of the employee? Did he have reasonable grounds for his belief? Did he investigate thoroughly and reasonably? Was the employee fairly given opportunity to explain?

CONSTRUCTIVE DISMISSAL

An employee who believes that his employer has made his working conditions so intolerable that it is impossible for him to continue to work for that employer can resign and claim to have been constructively dismissed. In effect the employee will have to show that the employer is in breach of a fundamental term of the contract of employment and has thereby entitled the employee to exercise his common law right to leave, with or without notice. From the employee's viewpoint timing is important. If he or she does not resign reasonably promptly, the breach may be said to have been affirmed and the employee will lose the right to go, claiming constructive dismissal in the process.

Telling an employee that a factory closure is likely at some *indefinite* time in the future, for example, does not give the employee the right to resign and claim constructive dismissal. But if the employer gives a date, and the employee leaves before that date, having given notice, his departure will most usually be labelled dismissal.

The employer who tells his employee that he must either resign or be dismissed, even though the employee resigns in the event, will discover that what he thought was a resignation will turn into a dismissal in the tribunal's hands. The same will be true if an employer extracts a resignation by supplying false information or by trickery.

PREGNANCY

It is probably fair to list pregnancy as an uncommon ground for dismissal – because it is almost always going to be deemed unfair. The protection given to pregnant women resides in our statutes and has been strengthened by the European Court of Justice. In effect *dismissal will be automatically unfair if it takes place because a woman is pregnant or for a reason connected with her pregnancy.*

So an employer cannot use pregnancy as a selection criterion in redundancy. But the inclusion of a pregnant woman within a group of employees selected for redundancy, say on the basis of last in, first out, would be unexceptionable. Whatever the criteria used, they must be applied generally.

The employer who engages a permanent replacement for an employee on maternity leave, even if he can show that he had no practical alternative, will find that he has dismissed unfairly. The reason was connected with her pregnancy.

Exceptionally, pregnant women may be dismissed and their dismissal *may* not be automatically unfair if:

- at the effective date of termination she is or will have become because of her pregnancy incapable of doing the work she is employed to do.
- because of her pregnancy she cannot or will not be able to continue after that date to do the work she is employed to do without contravention either by her or her employer of a duty or restriction imposed by or under any enactment.

In either case the employer is bound to offer an alternative job, if one is available. The alternative must be suitable and appropriate to her in the circumstances. The terms he offers must be no less favourable than before.

If no alternative is available, the employer must still establish that the dismissal was fair and reasonable. A tribunal would ask if he had acted reasonably, having regard to the size and administrative resources available to the employer. It would wish to see equity and reasonable behaviour on the part of the employer.

Conventionally, employers believe that it is possible to dismiss any employee within the first two years of the employee's service without the fear of such dismissal being called unfair. This is not necessarily true in the case of pregnant women. They may invoke our sex discrimination laws – and the European Court for that matter. Pleading reverse discrimination, on the grounds that men cannot become pregnant, is unlikely to work.

6

DISPUTED EXITS – ACAS AND THE TRIBUNAL

Departing employees, more often than not, have a pretty clear idea of their rights – and what they expect the employer to come up with in the severance package. The routine which involved a few gracious words, a tug of the forelock following the handover of a small bag of coins and a quick exit, is no more.

Today, the employee who believes he is being treated shabbily will react, using employment law as his means. The legal machinery exists. There is no shortage of sources of advice. The employee's union will help in this respect. Or there's always the Citizen's Advice Bureau if the solicitor route looks too expensive.

Whenever a tribunal case is involved, ACAS has a statutory duty to attempt to resolve disputes between employers and their staff. It is possible however to ask for ACAS help long before the threat of a tribunal case. It's worth looking at the less formal ways in which disputes may be settled.

PRIVILEGE
Any negotiations which take place through ACAS are privileged. That is to say that nothing can be revealed as to what has been said, or what was settled, or what the ACAS view of the circumstances might be.

Most businessmen are familiar with the phrase Without Prejudice. It tends to appear at the head of solicitors' letters when they are negotiating on their clients' behalf. In effect it implies that the contents of any offers they made cannot be subsequently revealed. There is no reason why employers and employees should not use this device in correspondence while dealing with each other directly in a dispute. The same doctrine can be applied, theoretically anyway, in conversation. It is difficult to prove after the event for obvious reasons. If a letter is marked Without Prejudice, there can be no argument.

The problem with Without Prejudice offers is that there is an implied acceptance of some sort of liability, however the writer protests. Thereafter, it seems to say, it is only a matter of price. The employer, most usually the offeror, believes himself to be saying something quite different. He is saying, to himself, that it is worth this much to save trouble and expense. But then, he would say that, wouldn't he?

For this reason it is usual for adjudicators, whether tribunals or courts, not to be told what has happened before the case is heard. Rarely it may be possible to reveal the contents of correspondence in this category. An example might lie in a case in which an employee had refused a reasonable Without Prejudice offer, had gone to a tribunal and been awarded substantially less than the sum offered originally. In these circumstances the tribunal can be shown the letter in question; and the employee may have costs awarded against him because the proceedings have been carried on unreasonably.

PRIVATE SETTLEMENTS

The gentlemanly settlement achieved prior to exit brings with it certain risks for the employer. As has been noted elsewhere, employment law tends to be weighted in favour of the employee – because the employer is reckoned to have more resources available than the employee.

Suppose for a moment that he wants to be rid of a senior employee but that he does not have grounds for fair dismissal. He can tell the employee that he wants him to go and offer him what the employer sees as a suitable severance package in return for his resignation. The employee may accept, even in writing, take the money and duly leave the company. Thereafter it is open to him to repudiate the agreement and bring a claim for unfair dismissal against the employer. Courts and tribunals will generally presume that he is entitled to do so, because he was not in a position to bargain effectively with his powerful ex-employer.

There is a way around this problem; and it involves ACAS. The deal can still be struck privately but the employer will make it clear that it is conditional on the employee signing a form of ACAS agreement which incorporates its terms. The ACAS conciliation officer will, on request, meet both parties, and ensure that they understand the significance of what is proposed. Thereafter he will produce an ACAS version of their agreement, (ACAS form COT3), which they will then sign. Once this signed document is in existence, neither side will have further recourse. It is fully binding on both parties. It's a safety net for both of them.

TRIBUNALS

Time limits

An employee claiming unfair dismissal must normally do so within three months. Unusually a tribunal might accept a longer period – say following a lay-off and promise of work at a later date which had not materialized in the event.

Constituents

Tribunals are independent courts, presided over by a legally qualified chairman. Two lay members sit with him or her – one drawn from the employers' side of industry, the other from the unions'. Most working days of the year will find about 60 tribunals sitting, in various parts of the country.

Style

The style is deliberately informal, although they will generally follow a normal court's procedure in relation to presentation of evidence. Happily however, they do not adhere slavishly to the Rules of Evidence: their approach is pragmatic.

Originating application

A technical term: used to identify the form lodged by the employee with the tribunal, representing his allegation of unfair dismissal. It must identify:

- the applicant.
- the employer (or the person or body against whom the proceedings are being brought).
- the outline of the nature of the claim or the relief sought.

Notice of Appearance

The form which the employer, (the respondent), must complete and return to the tribunal within 14 days. He must enter his defence therein, e.g. that he denies a redundancy claim because the employee was fired for incompetence and his position has been filled already.

Both parties should understand that there is no need, in an Originating Application or a Notice of Appearance, to *detail* the nature of the allegation or the defence. In fact if either party is relying on one substantive ground, they are unlikely to be allowed to switch to another in the course of a hearing: no matter how expedient it might seem.

The employer's check list

When a Notice of Appearance arrives the employer might consider whether:

- He needs external legal assistance. And the company's lawyers may not necessarily be the best place to go for it.

- He can respond intelligently within the 14 day period allowed. The employee's boss might be on holiday, for example. It is open to him to apply for a reasonable extension of time.
- The Originating Application contains insufficient information for him to be able to reply constructively. In these circumstances he will apply for an extension, quoting his reason, *and* apply at the same time to the Secretary of the Tribunal requiring the applicant to furnish further details of the grounds for his complaint and whatever supporting evidence he has.

   Clearly the employer cannot use this formula as a mere delaying tactic. He must underpin his requests with sound reasons as to why he cannot respond to the application in its original form.
- He believes honestly that he has no case to answer. In these circumstances he can apply for a *pre-hearing assessment* to the Secretary of the Tribunals. If he succeeds in getting one, both parties will be allowed to produce further evidence in writing to add to what the tribunal already knows. The outcome might be that the employee would be told that his case had little or no chance of success; and that, if he went forward with it, he might get stuck with costs against him. Conversely, the employer might fail at this stage: in which event he would be best advised to settle out of court as soon as he can.

Conciliation

The ACAS conciliation officer will get in touch with both parties to a dispute before the date set for their appearance before the tribunal. He is bound to do so by statute. It is his duty to act as honest broker and try to settle the dispute without the need for a formal hearing. He will look at what each side has said thus far and talk to them about their likely chances of what they might see as success in the hands of a tribunal. He'll try to inject realism into the proceedings: to defuse what might be an emotional situation on either or both sides.

In the process, he does not take sides. The ACAS conciliation officer will invariably be highly experienced in industrial relations and used to dealing with shop floor employees and very senior executives – and anyone in between. His success rate tends to be very high. Once a compromise has been reached, he will prepare the ACAS form COT3 referred to earlier. As before, once both parties have signed it, they are bound by this agreement. There can be no further recourse.

Preparation for appearance

Once an employer is committed to appearing before a tribunal he will recognise that he must prepare carefully. The checklist which follows may be useful:

- *Facts*: assemble them, including witnesses' statements and any corroborating evidence.
- *Documentary evidence*: put the dossier together; and remember that it might include:
  - employee's contract of employment
  - employee's job description
  - formal warnings, other relevant letters and memos
  - training records, formal appraisals
  - company's disciplinary procedure and rules
  - company's letter dismissing employee
  - statement of reasons for dismissal
  - evidence of employee's current rewards

Preparation does not end here. Both parties will have met the ACAS conciliation officer and should have an understanding of the issues involved. The employer, for his part, must address these issues. He'll need to be thoroughly objective in reviewing his position. He may be well advised to do some research: the local reference library is usually most helpful. There is merit in developing the arguments he will put forward and in trying to anticipate what the applicant will say – and what potentially embarrassing questions he might ask at the hearing.

It is open to the employee to ask the company, via the tribunal, to produce documents and information. This process, known as Discovery of documents, will depend on the employee being specific. Fishing trips are not allowed. Only if the information he or she wants is relevant and fairly easily accessible, would the tribunal require the employer to produce it.

7

OUTPLACEMENT

Outplacement organizations set out to provide counselling, advice on job finding, interview techniques and
a number of other services to redundant employees. A
few may offer to find jobs for the individuals involved –
as distinct from advising them how to become prof-
icient at getting a job for themselves.

These organizations have been around for many years.
In the recent and current recession they have grown in
number and size. It must be one of the fastest growing
sectors. Generally, but not always, the employer pays
for their services. It's worth looking at why an
employer might choose to use them, what they do, the
difficult problem of choosing the right one; and what
the costs are likely to be.

Benefits to the employer

- It labels him as caring and sympathetic as an individual and as representing the company. It's good
  PR on both fronts, internally and externally.
- It helps, in part at least, to cushion the shock to the
  redundant employee, who is given fresh hope and a
  focus. If he or she is serving out notice, morale will
  be improved.
- It will save executive time. The outplacement
  organization's counsellors will provide the emotional support and practical advice that otherwise
  might have had to be supplied by the company's
  executives.
- It reduces any perceived need, whether stemming
  from feelings of guilt or not, to offer an over-
  generous settlement. Instead the employee is being
  offered what he really wants – the prospect of
  another job.

- If an outplacement organization is engaged *before* the redundancy is declared, it can help the executive concerned to plan how to deal with what can be a sensitive, awkward and embarrassing process.
- Large numbers of people may be made redundant at the same time. A centralized outplacement service based at the employer's premises can provide practical help in getting new jobs for those involved. It will do no harm to the employer's continuing relationship with the union either.
- Pragmatically, the manager who knows that his employer provides an effective outplacement package will be less reluctant to make tough decisions involving, say, the closure of uneconomical units.

What they do

There's considerable variety within the menus available. To a large extent, variations tend to be related to size. There are probably fewer than ten sizeable companies in the business, possibly another twenty or so in the middle and a host of small outfits, including many one-man consultancies. Most will expect redundant managers to use their premises as a base but distance learning – or what looks something like learning to cope with redundancy largely by post – has emerged as a recent alternative.

The range of services offered includes

COUNSELLING

Probably the most important element of any package in this area. It is doubtful whether it can be done as well by correspondence as by an experienced and sympathetic counsellor in person.

It has been suggested that redundant staff commonly experience a series of emotions, beginning with shock, then rage, followed by a desire for revenge and, subsequently, despair. Only thereafter do they climb out of the trough and begin to focus constructively on the process of getting a new job.

The counsellor's task in part is to get them through these early stages. Some counsellors believe that they must advise the participant's partner too. Beyond the initial trauma there will be a need for encouragement, for reassurance and confidence building; and maybe even a little gentle bullying from time to time. The counsellor's role is not an easy one. In at least one major consultancy, counsellors are told that they may unload the effects on them of the accumulated emotion they are exposed to onto the in-house psychologist at regular intervals. Presumably the poor psychologist goes to another psychologist.

PSYCHOMETRIC TESTING/CAREER GUIDANCE

Reputable outplacement organizations will have at their disposal a range of tests from which they will select what is appropriate in individual cases. Many employers will be familiar with testing as a selection aid. In the outplacement context testing, used intelligently, may uncover the fact that, for a major part of his working life a man has been doing work for which he is quite unsuited: that he has skills, whether social or technical, which could be used to best advantage in a totally different area.

Beyond this sort of dramatic discovery, testing will be used to enable the redundant employee to understand himself, his strengths and his weaknesses. To this extent many of the selection tests will continue to be appropriate. It is important though that the results of testing are analysed by a trained occupational psychologist: the lay interpretation may be little better than a trip to the fortune-teller's tent.

Test results and their inter-relationships are best conveyed to the subject by the psychologist, who will need to maintain a delicate balance between getting the participant to understand what he is and what he has to offer – and not destroying his self-confidence in the process. The format for their discussion might be:

- Intellectual effectiveness: he'll be told which group he is being compared with and thereafter be given an indication of his ability in relation to numerical, verbal, logical and imaginative problems.
- His work approach: under the headings of, say, mastery of detail, productivity, quality of work, decision making, tolerance for pressure, flexibility, ambition.
- Relationships: with superiors, peers and subordinates.
- Primary assets: a summary of key points.
- Primary limitations: ditto.
- Development guidelines: a definition of the environment he needs and the ways in which he can develop, or sometimes modify, his style and approach.
- Summary: What is he now? Where might he go from here?

RESEARCH AND ADMIN FACILITIES

The more sophisticated outplacement organizations recognize that making office space available for the use of redundant executives serves a number of useful purposes. The redundant executive hasn't got a secretary any more. If he cannot use a word processor himself, a member of staff will produce letters and type CVs for him. If he needs to research a sector or a company, the reference books or computer-based information are readily available.

Beyond this, because the individual will have lost the reassurance of the routine of going to the office each day and the social comfort it gave him, going to the out-placement offices instead is at least part substitute. Meeting fellow sufferers there allows social contact which might be missing otherwise.

JOB SEARCH TRAINING

A large proportion of participants find themselves at sea when faced, perhaps for the first time in their lives, with the need to find a new job. They will be shown how to construct a well thought out CV and may practise writing letters of application. They'll be taught the principles of networking, i.e. using contacts, and their network of contacts in turn, to meet people who might help them to find a job – on the basis that many more jobs are filled each year via this route than ever appear in advertisements.

At the same time they'll see the dummy interviews they have taken part in replayed to them on closed-circuit television. They will try to anticipate and rehearse the answers to awkward questions they might be asked.

THE JOB CLUB

Perhaps because it has become so much more common in recent years, the stigma which used to attach to the word redundant has all but disappeared. Management selection and recruitment consultants now look upon some of the more reputable and efficient outplacement organizations as useful sources of potential candidates. They will feed them details of selected vacancies, many of which will not be generally advertised. The recruitment consultant is well aware, for example, that if his client wants an older, mature manager, the outplacement resource is likely to be very useful on occasion.

The more effective outplacement offices contain what

amounts to a clearing house in which these opportunities can be matched with potential candidates. Candidates are encouraged to study the bulletins issued, to look at notice boards and to talk to each other about what they have done or intend to do. This interchange is important. It creates a club atmosphere among people with a shared interest. The members will learn from each other as well as from their counsellors.

COSTS

The outplacement company with large, plush offices in the West End of London and equally plush branches in all major cities is likely to charge more than the one-man business. That's obvious: the larger organization would of course argue that it gives more. It is difficult to generalize but many of the larger outfits would expect up to 20 per cent of the redundant employee's former salary level. There may be extras too: some would expect additional fees for CV preparation and an extended guarantee as it were, i.e. after-care continuing for six months or more beyond the initial period. Many will give volume discounts if they are asked to take on a batch of ex-employees.

Blue collar outplacement following, for example, a factory closure, would involve setting up a counselling and clearing facility on the employer's premises. Since mobility is likely to be limited, other local employers will be made aware of the pool of labour now available. Individuals will be given advice on State benefits, investment of redundancy pay and so on. There are no fixed rates in this area. Employers should get competitive quotations – after they have checked on individual past performance: price isn't everything.

Many of these organizations will suggest that they can tailor their programmes to meet the employer's needs. What this means generally is that they will tailor to meet his purse. In effect they will offer to provide a reduced service for less money. In many instances the employee is at the mercy of the employer. If outplacement is presented to him as a grace and favour exit bonus, he may find it difficult to argue that he needs the full service. Indeed the employer may offer a cunning compromise by suggesting that any marginal cost must come from his settlement. There is little point in taking a moral stance here. But employers might do well to remember that more actions for unfair dismissal have probably been brought by employees who resented the manner of their dismissal than by those concerned with the amount of their settlements.

CHOICE

One he has identified a pool of established, reputable outplacement consultants, via the Federation of Recruitment & Employment Services, (F.R.E.S., 36–38 Mortimer Street, London W1N 7RB, tel 071 323 4300) or the Institute of Personnel Management, these are the questions the employer must ask about each organization:

- How long has it existed?
- What is its track record – what proportion of their participants found jobs within, say six months
    (Try asking for it by age group: younger people are always easier to place)
- Are its offices within easy reach?
- What research facilities do they provide for candidates?
- Is there a limit on the secretarial help they give?
- Is there an overall time limit anyway?
- Are there extra costs – for CV help for example?
- Do they test? Is there a resident psychologist, or an external one they use conventionally?
- Do they provide crisis counselling? Are they able to provide counselling to partners if necessary?

- What facilities exist for interview training and practice?
- What is the ratio of consultants to participants? (note: not *staff* but *consultants*. Some organizations overload their consultants. They cannot function effectively with a case load of 40: 10 or 12 is likely to be the maximum number.)
- How good is their own network? Do recruitment consultants and employers come to them? How many jobs did they fill this way last year?
- Do they get paid by the new employer when they supply a successful candidate? Ethically they shouldn't: there is a direct conflict of interest. If they do, avoid them.
- Have you visited the premises and talked to consultants and users?
- Finally, what does it cost?

As noted earlier, it is likely that more people sue or go to tribunals because of the way in which they have been dismissed than because they feel that the settlement offered was inadequate. There are some obvious do's and don'ts which are listed below. If it will make the hard-hearted finance man feel any better about it, they are based on pragmatism rather than any desire to take the moral high ground.

REDUNDANCY PROCEDURE

Typically, in large companies, ACAS will recommend the preparation, before the event, of a general policy statement, after consultation with the union if appropriate. It might include:

- an introductory statement of intent towards maintaining job security wherever practicable
- details of consultation arrangements
- measures for avoiding or minimizing compulsory redundancies
- the selection criteria to be used where redundancy is unavoidable
- details of the severance terms
- the company's policy in relation to helping redundant employees to obtain training or in their search for a new job

This routine is obviously more likely to be followed in large companies. It does have the merit of removing uncertainty however.

TIMING

It's best to give employees a definite leaving date. It is mistaken kindness to try to sugar the pill with deliberately vague indications founded on the hope that the individual will solve management's problem by finding a new job quickly. He or she may not be able to, no matter how hard they try. Or, if the predicted event seems far enough off or even unreal, they may not try too hard anyway.

The more senior the employee, the longer it is likely to take to find a new job. The more notice given, the better.

There's no need to fire the employee on his or her birthday, or on the day before they are due to go on holiday. If there are any other events lurking around which are known about – a 25th wedding anniversary perhaps – they can be avoided with a little planning and thought.

JOB SEARCH

An employee under notice ought to be given opportunity to search for a new job and attend interviews as necessary. Particularly at senior levels, payment in lieu of notice is common. Apart from any other consideration, it is highly tax-effective from the employee's standpoint. If the senior manager involved has had a company car it's a good idea to let him keep it, at least until the theoretical period of notice expires, possibly for longer. The additional cost to the company is usually minimal: though it might be prudent to require the employee to pay for his own petrol.

Employers will sometimes go to quite extraordinary lengths, at a redundant manager's request, to create and preserve an illusion that he or she is still employed by the company when, in fact, they were made redundant months earlier. Switchboards will be instructed to refer calls to 'his secretary' who will take messages, explain that he is out of the office but that she can get him to return the call later in the day.

This is a charade and serves no useful purpose whatsoever. It usually begins with the commonly held belief that it is easier to get a new job if one is seen to be working when one applies. It has its roots too in the idea that some awful stigma attaches to the word redundancy. This may have been so, ten or twenty years ago. Today it is untrue. Thousands of managers, tens of thousands of employees, have been made redundant. It is silly to suppose that they were all thrown out of their jobs because they were no good at them. When a recruiting manager looks at a CV and discovers that an applicant was made redundant, his reaction is likely to be, first, 'there, but for the grace of God, go I,' and, second, 'Good. At least this one will be available quickly'.

By all means employers should offer secretarial help, in the production of CVs for example. This is helpful. If outplacement is being provided, even this will be unnecessary. But they ought to encourage their ex-managers to come clean. Recruitment consultants are used to CVs which seem to indicate that candidate X is currently with company Y – because the space where a final date should appear has, cunningly, been left blank. Their opening question is almost always, 'Tell me, are you still with Y?'

FRINGE BENEFITS

Cars and private health cover

Management rewards packages will commonly include a range of fringe benefits. The company car has been mentioned already. Let the manager hang on to it for a reasonable period. Or sell it to him at some sort of preferential price. He or she may well have had private health cover which extended to the immediate family. Subscriptions tend to be paid annually in advance. Clawing back the unexpired portion isn't going to swell the coffers much. Take the opportunity to relieve at least one anxiety by continuing cover, once again for a reasonable period.

Life cover and pensions

It may be possible to continue to provide life and accident cover under the employer's existing arrangements for a few months after severance. It may be a little more complicated if life cover is an element of the company's pension plan and therefore depends on membership. The company's pension advisers or insurance brokers will help however. If all else fails, the latter will usually be pleased to provide quotations for interim cover.

The employer's pension fund may represent occasional opportunity for employer and employee alike, depending on the age and length of membership of the employee in question. Early retirement may be a practical alternative to redundancy. It is of course possible to augment an early retirement pension. The actuaries to the fund may or may not expect the company to pay a lump sum into the fund to compensate for augmentation. But if the employer knows that his fund is in surplus and expects to take a contribution holiday next year – or whenever – his view as to the amount involved might be quite sanguine.

Consultancy

In certain circumstances it may be feasible to provide a guarantee of consultancy work within the organization, over a given period, following either redundancy or early retirement. It will supplement the individual's income on the one hand and lessen the pangs of severance on the other. Apart from the economic aspects, there's a lot to be said for the maintenance of social contact. In fact, for someone no longer young, who may perhaps find it very difficult to get a new job, it is important that he or she should feel needed: that what they have to offer is still valuable.

As a fill-in between severance and when a pension becomes available it may be particularly useful. The employer ought to ensure, though, that the tasks involved are real. The ex-employee won't want charity.

References

If an outplacement organization is involved they'll see it as part of their task to agree the form of reference the employer is going to give if asked. Their intervention may be most useful when employer and employee have not parted on the best of terms. They will agree a form of words with the employer. He will undertake to use this form invariably. There is no formal agreement: merely an understanding between the three parties. Generally, it works: perhaps because the employer wants to show the outplacement people that he is an honourable man and not in the least petty.

In the absence of intermediaries – presuming no ill will – it is an issue the employer ought to tackle during the tidying up process. The easiest way to do it is to ask the employee to draft his or her own reference and, if it isn't outrageous, to use it.

Survivors

It's easy to forget all about the people who are left behind. Their concerns might include:

- Guilt at having survived
- Jealousy: they'll be aware that some attractive settlements have been made. And that some of the people involved walked straight into new jobs.
- Fear: when is it going to be their turn?
- Outrage: there didn't seem to be much fairness or even sense in the selection for redundancy criteria.
- Mistrust: management cannot now be trusted, whatever they say.
- Inadequacy: the extent and requirements of individual jobs has been increased. Can they cope?
- Culture: the company culture has changed dramatically. Will they like the new one? Can they survive it?

Organizations tend to go into shock following redundancies of any significant size. They will recover, of course; the memory dims. But waiting for the eventual recovery is not management – other than management by default. Meanwhile morale will have suffered. A loss of confidence may result in some of the better employees finding themselves jobs elsewhere. The American philosophy 'if it aint broke, don't mend it' is sensible in some circumstances. Not this time though. It's broke, so management had better do something about it.

The solution will vary according to size, type and style of organization. There cannot be a general rule. The key must be communication – with opportunity for employees to discuss what has happened with and to ask questions of senior management.

SAMPLE DISCIPLINARY PROCEDURE

Every employer should have a formal, written procedure. Its existence provides protection for employer and employee. Tribunals and courts look kindly upon employers who have produced one – and have stuck to its rules.

The sample given below presumes that a recognized union exists within the company.

General

1. The maintenance of high standards of behaviour and performance is necessary for the efficient operation of the company. This statement sets down the procedures to be followed in dealing with matters of internal company discipline.
2. Employees acting contrary to their terms and conditions of employment of the best interest of the company will be the subject of disciplinary action taken in accordance with the procedures and principles laid down herein.

Scope

3. All employees of Company X Limited and its subsidiaries are covered by this procedure. All employees are expected to be aware of their terms and conditions of employment and the accepted standards of conduct within the company. Management is responsible for explaining company rules, conditions of employment and the standards of conduct expected of employees.

Types of offence

4. Disciplinary offences have been categorized into two types for the purposes of this statement. These are:

    (i) General misconduct
    (ii) Serious misconduct

5. Offences committed under these categories will be dealt with in accordance with the procedures laid out below and may result in an oral warning, a written warning, suspension, demotion, down-grading or dismissal with or without notice depending upon the circumstances of the case.

General misconduct

6. The term general misconduct means breaches of company rules, conditions of employment or un-satisfactory performance of any nature not more particularly covered by the term serious misconduct defined in the appropriate section set out below. Where management believes that the employee has acted in such a way that requires disciplinary action to be taken, the procedure to be adopted will be as follows:-

    (i) The employee's departmental head will bring the attention of the employee to the breach. He may issue an oral warning identifying the breach and suggesting ways in which the employee's conduct or performance may be improved. The head of department will note that an oral warning has been given, specifying the date and the nature of the breach.

    (ii) On a repetition of the offence or an offence of a related character the head of department shall interview the employee and will detail the nature of the repetition. The employee will receive a written warning which shall be recorded on his personal file specifying the nature of the offence and the date on which the written warning was given together with appropriate comments as to the need for improvement. The written warning will also state the consequences of any repetition of the offence including dismissal of the employee or other action (such as a transfer to an alternative job) as appropriate.

(iii) Further repetition of the particular offence or of an offence of a related character may result in the dismissal of the employee.

7. An employee may seek to have a written warning removed from his or her personal record after 12 months service without any repetition of the original or a similar offence.

Serious misconduct

8. Serious misconduct may render an employee liable to instant dismissal without notice. Examples of the sorts of offences considered to be serious misconduct are:-

- Falsification of records
- Disregard of safety rules or precautions
- Theft from another employee or the company
- Abuse of another employee's or the company's property
- Assault upon another employee
- Fighting
- Drunkenness or the use of drugs
- Refusal to carry out a reasonable instruction

9. The above list is not an exhaustive or an inclusive list. Where an offence of this nature has been committed the employee concerned will be interviewed immediately by a senior member of

management and the circumstances of the case will be fully discussed. In some instances it may be necessary to suspend the employee with pay to allow details of the incident to be investigated fully.

10. The employee may elect to have present a union representative and if appropriate may call witnesses at any stage of the disciplinary procedure.

11. If management is satisfied that the employee has committed serious misconduct having heard evidence from all relevant parties, disciplinary action will be taken and dismissal may result.It shall be open to management in these circumstances to impose suspension, demotion or downgrading or dismissal with or without notice depending upon the circumstances of the case.

Conduct of proceedings

12. Management has the right to seek information from any employee to ensure that the fullest investigation is carried out and the employee has the right if he so wishes to be represented by his union and to call evidence from other employees on his own behalf and to be told of the nature of the complaint made against him.

Ratification

13. Any decision to dismiss, downgrade, suspend or demote must be ratified before the event by a director of the company.

Appeal

14. In the event of an employee disputing any disciplinary action it is open to him or her to appeal to the next highest level of management. In cases of

general misconduct any warning or penalty shall only become effective once the appeal procedure has been carried through. In cases of serious misconduct where dismissal is in train any appeal must be made as soon as notice of dismissal has been given. Such appeals will be heard by the next senior level of management within the next working day. When for any reason the appeal cannot be heard within this period the effect of the decision to dismiss will be deferred until the appeal has been heard. It is open to an employee finally to appeal to the board of directors of the company.

Date   Signed ....

        Position ....

APPENDIX

STATUTES AND REGULATIONS
Employment Acts 1980, 1982, 1988, 1989, 1990
Employment Protection Act 1975
Employment Protection (Consolidation) Act 1978
Industrial Relations Act 1971
Sex Discrimination Act 1986
Transfer of Undertakings (Protection of
    Employment) Regulations 1981
Access to Medical Reports Act 1988
Employment Appeal Tribunal Rules 1980
Employment Appeal Tribunal (Amendment) Rules
    1985

C
APPENDIX

RECOMMENDED FURTHER READING

Bowers, J. and Goraj, A. *Blackstone's Annual Update '91 – Employment Law*, London: Blackstone

Fagan, N. *Contracts of Employment*, London: Sweet & Maxwell

Morris, S. *Handling Redundancy*, London: Industrial Society Press

Waud, C. *Employment Law*, London: Chapmans

INDEX

Also published by Century Business

HOW TO NEGOTIATE YOUR SALARY
Tips, gambits and strategies for getting the package you deserve

ALAN JONES

Everything you need to know to enter into salary discussions confident of gaining the total remuneration package (TRP) that you want and deserve.

Whether negotiating a salary for a new job or requesting a pay rise in a current job, this is the ideal guide if you feel that your negotiation skills could benefit from some fine-tuning.

Complete with action checklists and practical examples, *How to Negotiate Your Salary* is another readable and effective book from the author of *How to Write a Winning CV* and *How to Build a Successful Career*.

Alan Jones is a leading outplacement consultant and freelance writer.

Paperback £7.99
208 pp   216 x 135 mm
0712653910

MAKING A COMEBACK

A woman's guide to returning to work after a break

MARGARET KORVING

The message is clear – there has never been a better time for women returning to work. A sharp decline in school-leavers means that employers are turning to previously ignored 'minorities' – like working mothers and the young retired – to meet the skills shortages that now threaten them.

But just how easy is it to step back on to the career ladder after a long period spent bringing up your children or caring for elderly relatives – a period in which technology has changed the workplace out of all recognition? How do you develop a career and keep your family content? What provisions, in terms of child care and training opportunities, are really being made by employers and government to entice women back into full-time careers?

Making A Comeback examines in detail the recent changes in prospects for women returners. It looks at what is on offer, and gives down-to-earth advice on how to select, train for and secure a new and exciting career – without neglecting your home or family.

Margaret Korving is one of Britain's most popular and experienced careers experts. She was careers consultant to the *Daily Telegraph* for 18 years.

Paperback £5.99
136 pp   216 x 135 mm
0091744156

HOW TO READ THE FINANCIAL PAGES

A simple guide to the way money works and the jargon

MICHAEL BRETT

This is an expanded, third edition of the bestselling and definitive guide to the City of London, its markets and how they are written up in the financial pages. The book has been fully revised to include all the radical changes that have taken place in the City since Big Bang, and covers among other topics the interlocking and interacting worlds of the gilt-edged markets, the money market and the ERM.

Anyone who needs to understand the language of finance and the markets will find this book essential. A permanent fixture on Top Ten Business Bookseller lists, it strips away the jargon and mystique cloaking much of the City's activity and explains clearly how to 'read between the lines' of financial pages and reports.

Michael Brett, former editor of *Investors Chronicle*, is a financial journalist and lecturer at City University.

Paperback £8.99
312 pp   216 x 135 mm
0091748895

HOW TO BE HEADHUNTED

The art of building and sustaining your professional reputation

YVONNE SARCH

'Headhunting', or using the services of an executive search consultant, is now big business. Mergers, acquisitions and buyouts are commonplace, leading to a rapid turnover of top executives. In an increasing number of cases, such executives do not need to look for new organizations – the organizations find them.

But how do these sought-after high-flyers create such a flattering and rewarding demand for themselves? Are they simply the most able, hard-working and attractive people in their fields, or do they consciously adopt a detailed strategy for making themselves visible; for getting themselves and their achievements noticed by the 'right' people?

Written by one of Britain's top executive consultants (who was herself headhunted for her present top position), *How to be Headhunted* is a frank and authoritative guide to developing your professional profile and your career – both inside and outside the office. Aimed specifically at those who already have the qualifications, experience and ambition necessary for the jobs they want, it shows how to develop the self-worth, charisma and reputation demanded by professional recruiters.

Yvonne Sarch is a director of SSI, a major executive search firm.

Paperback £7.99
240 pp   234 x 153 mm
0712698957

GETTING TO YES

Negotiating agreement without giving in

ROGER FISHER & WILLIAM URY

A completely revised, second edition of the book recognized worldwide as the most effective guide to the negotiation game.

Successful negotiation is a core component of individual achievement. *Getting to Yes* provides practical strategies for getting what you want while keeping your adversaries happy. Its powerful, easily mastered principles will see you through no matter what the other side resorts to!

This edition includes a new introduction and many new examples, as well as the authors' answers to the ten most commonly asked questions about *Getting to Yes*.

A vitally important book for anyone dealing with other people in business, politics, diplomacy or counselling.

Roger Fisher is Williston Professor of Law at Harvard Law School and Director of the Harvard Negotiation Project. **William Ury** is a specialist in negotiation and Associate Director of the Harvard Negotiation Project.

Paperback £5.99
176 pp   198 x 126 mm
071265528X

GETTING PAST NO

Negotiating with difficult people

WILLIAM URY

A sequel to all-time bestseller *Getting to Yes,* this new book
from international negotiation guru William Ury tackles the
very thorniest aspect of the subject: dealing with people who
won't deal.

What if the other side doesn't *want* to get to yes?

What if their answer is no? How do you negotiate with such
difficult people?

William Ury has simplified and distilled the techniques of
negotiation with unwilling adversaries into five basic and
universal principles, illustrated with a host of examples and
techniques on which to draw in difficult situations. Whether
your opponents are obstructive, offensive or downright
deceptive, *Getting Past No* provides success strategies for
everyone who has to negotiate: businesspeople, lawyers,
politicians, diplomats and trade union leaders.

William Ury is an internationally recognized expert on
negotiation and Associate Director of the Harvard
Negotiation Project.

Paperback £5.99
164 pp   198 x 126 mm
0712655239